Drinking
Problem
?

Drinking Problem?

JOHN E. KELLER

Fortress Press   Philadelphia

Library of Congress Catalog Card Number 75-133036
ISBN 0-8006-0155-6

Fourteenth printing 1987

3191H87   Printed in the United States of America   1-155

Series Introduction

Pocket Counsel Books are intended to help people with problems in a specific way. Problems may arise in connection with family life, marriage, grief, alcoholism, drugs or death. In addressing themselves to these and similar problems, the authors have made every effort to speak in language free from technical vocabulary.

Because these books are not only nontechnical but also brief, they offer a good start in helping people with specific problems. Face-to-face conversation between counselor and counselee is a necessary part of the help the authors envision through these books. The books are not a substitute for person-to-person counseling: they supplement counseling.

As the reader gets into a book dealing with his concerns, he will discover that the author aims at opening up areas of inquiry for further reflection. Thus through what is being read that which needs to be said and spoken out loud may come to the surface in dialog with the counselor. In "working through" a given problem in this personal way, help may come.

WILLIAM E. HULME
General Editor

Contents

1.

The
Key
Question

If you have any questions about your drinking, this book is for you. If someone else is concerned about your drinking, even though you are not, you may want to read these pages to find out if there is anything that gives them, and should give you, good reason to be concerned. If, on the other hand, it is not your drinking but someone else's that troubles you, this book may help you to understand that person's drinking.

This book is not intended to make you or anyone else quit drinking. Whether somebody drinks or not is his own business and his own responsibility. If you want to keep on drinking, this book won't interfere with that. My purpose is simply to help you to understand and determine what the nature of a serious drinking problem is and what can be done about it.

In all honesty, however, I must add that if you have a real drinking problem but don't yet know it, this book will inevitably enlarge your understanding and thus also significantly spoil your drinking. It will never seem quite the same again.

The place to begin is not with what somebody else may be thinking and saying about your drinking, but with what you are thinking and saying about it to yourself and, most important, how you are feeling about it. You may be asking yourself some questions, and that is the best way to start the journey toward understanding.

How is it with you? How do you—all alone within yourself—feel about your drinking? Do you think it isn't really a problem, but find yourself wondering at times about it? Do you feel that sometimes you drink too much, but your drinking isn't as serious as someone else might think? Is there anything specific about your drinking that does concern you—anything at all? If so, what is it? When did this first begin to evidence itself—how many weeks, or months, or years ago? Whatever this is, why does it concern you? Assuming that you don't believe there is anything wrong with drinking per se, assuming that you have been drinking for a while and that for some time there was nothing about it that particularly concerned you, what is it now? What has changed? How are you in any way drinking differently than you used to? What kind of an explanation for this change have you come up with? Does your explanation satisfy you? If you think it does, why do you think it still concerns you?

What is it? Are you drinking more frequently? Has the amount you drink significantly increased? Do you find yourself sometimes drinking beyond your own intention—beyond the amount you wanted to drink? Do you find yourself trying to curb your drinking but not being successful at it? Do you find yourself drinking at times when you feel you shouldn't be drinking? Do you find yourself going on the water wagon, feeling that something has happened to your drinking that makes you want to prove to yourself that you can take it or leave it? What is the longest period you have gone without drinking too much in the last year? Do any of these concern you?

Is drinking beginning to cause difficulties in your marriage? Are you spending more money on drinking than you really feel you should or can afford? Is drinking causing problems in your work? Has your drinking had any effect on what you think of yourself, your self-respect? Do you feel any differently toward the person you see in the mirror? Do any of these concern you?

These are just a few possibilities. There are any number of reasons why a person might be concerned about his drinking, and we will be discussing many others at a later stage. The main point about the reasons given is that they are not only quite common but also very real and important. They are not something to be dismissed or glossed over as trivial and insignificant. It would take an insensitive person to be indifferent to reasons like these. So if you are concerned, you are someone who is sensitive, who will want to understand more about his or her drinking.

Your concern does not stop with asking yourself a few questions and then putting them out of your head. Your mind and feelings don't work that way. If you are concerned because of any of the reasons mentioned, you have undoubtedly also been thinking about your drinking, wondering about it, trying to figure it out, even feeling guilty about it, and also possibly trying to change it. Chances are that at the same time you have also been denying it, minimizing it, excusing it, blaming others for it, or trying to prove that there is really nothing to be worried about. That is what people often do when they have a problem they either don't understand or aren't yet quite ready to face. Perhaps you are concerned enough right now so that you are willing to see whether or not you really have a serious drinking problem.

Before going any further let's clarify what we are going to be talking about. We are not going to be saying much about drinking itself. Alcoholic beverages are available everywhere, and they are being consumed. People drink or don't drink for all kinds of reasons, some of them healthy and some unhealthy. Some drink very little, some are heavy drinkers. No matter what their reasons, many such people never have any difficulties because of drinking. In this sense it is no problem. It is just drinking.

Besides drinking, there is drunkenness. Some people who drink never get drunk. But many others do at times drink themselves drunk—not all the time, not most of the time, but sometimes. People get drunk for a variety of reasons—to "have a good time," to celebrate, or to forget for the moment some recent unhappy experience. Sometimes a person who gets drunk may end up in some sort of trouble through a social blunder, an accident, a ticket for drunken driving. But in most cases of such drunkenness, the important thing is that it is a self-willed phenomenon. It happens because the person decides to drink himself into drunkenness.

There is another kind of drinking, however, that is somewhat different from and more than simple drunkenness. It is *problem drinking*. This is drinking, usually to excess, in order to escape from some basic problems in living. It goes beyond the use of alcohol to forget a momentary difficulty or an upsetting experience. Drinking is perceived and used as a way out of a deeper and more persistent problem. Rather than face the problems directly and work them through, the person tries to "solve" them by turning to alcohol.

In the forms of drinking we have talked about up to this point, there is one common element. There is still the inner freedom, the willpower if you prefer, to choose not to drink, or to drink in moderation. Even the problem drinker could decide to face up to his difficulties and do something realistic about them. He could—suddenly or gradually—"come to his senses" and realize that drinking is no solution. He still has the freedom to control or quit his drinking and to learn how to cope with his problems.

One of the decisions you will have to make as you think it over is whether yours is problem drinking. Only you can answer the question, for it is your own life situation that gives the evidence. It may be, if your drinking has given you real concern for some time, that you would be quite ready to describe it as problem drinking.

There is another form of drinking for you to consider that can include the others—simple drinking, drunkenness, and problem drinking—but goes beyond them. The crucial difference was aptly expressed by a woman who said: "I used to drink because I had problems, but now I have a *drinking problem*."

It does not sound as though there is much of a difference between the two—problem drinking and drinking problem. But that simple reversal of words contains a key that marks off one whole world from another. The entire focus is changed. There is a difference in quality between a drinking problem and the other forms. It is no longer simple drinking because it increasingly, and soon inevitably, ends up in drunkenness. It has ceased to be mere drunkenness because the drinking into drunkenness is no longer done with intention. And it is not problem drinking because even if the problems were resolved the excessive drinking would continue.

4

That last sentence sounds ridiculous. We know that, but we also know it is true. Whatever you think about it or however you find yourself reacting to it, don't dismiss it too quickly. There is the possibility that this could provide you with an answer to a question about your drinking that has so far gone unanswered.

Let's look a little further at problem drinking and a drinking problem. People who start drinking more frequently and in greater amounts because they are trying to run away from their problems obviously do not eliminate or solve them. But drinking does for a while remove the pain and reality.

Here is a man who feels dominated by his wife. This makes him angry. He may not even let himself know he's angry. If he is aware of his feelings he keeps them inside or he may even express them. In either case, he really doesn't get rid of his anger. It stays with him. So he seeks to escape the reality of his problem by deciding to go out and get drunk. This is problem drinking.

Within a relatively short period of time, he realizes that getting drunk isn't the answer. He decides to face reality and do something about his problem—get help, if necessary.

Or here is a woman fifty-five years old. She has drunk all of her adult life, quite moderately and with control. Lately she has begun to feel as if she has been left all alone. The children have left home. She no longer feels needed. Her husband is still active in his business. She is beginning to feel he doesn't really care. She is lonely. She feels sorry for herself. She starts drinking by herself at home to anesthetize the pain of these feelings. This is problem drinking.

Then one day this woman decides that it is silly to sit around feeling sorry for herself. She accepts the reality of her life. She becomes active in volunteer work and social activities. She becomes a helping person. She no longer sits at home with a glass in her hand. Whenever she gets those feelings, and she knows she will get them again, she is not going to turn to drinking because she realizes that it never helped solve anything. She has her problems and prefers to recognize them and do something about them.

The point in these two stories is this: If these people decide to face their problems and do something about them, they can quit their problem drinking and go back to drinking the way they used to—if they want to. They can also decide to quit drinking altogether if they want to, and that will not be difficult. You may know people who have changed their drinking habits this way.

But the problem drinking of either of these two people could easily have become a drinking problem. By then, in spite of what they would have thought about doing or actually would have done in regard to their problems, the excessive drinking would have continued. The difference would be that there would be loss of control over alcohol. You no longer control your drinking. It controls you.

What, then, is loss of control? It is first evidenced by the inability to drink according to one's own intention. It is being unable to know or predict "How much will I end up drinking if I take that first drink." It is the inability to control consistently the amount one will drink.

Consider the case of a man who has had some drinking episodes that he can't really explain satisfactorily to himself. He has given himself plausible reasons or explanations and has acted as though they are sufficient. He has tried to give an explanation for staying at the bar from four o'clock in the afternoon until ten-thirty at night, missing dinner and not calling his wife: "Well, you know how it is, Joe buys a drink, you buy a drink, Bill buys a drink. . . ." But deep inside he knows this isn't good enough because he knows that Joe and Bill left the bar, caught the train and were home for dinner. Or if Joe and Bill were still there at ten-thirty, he knows that they aren't the same men he used to drink with. He has changed his drinking companions to be with those who now drink more the way he does.

He really has no satisfactory explanation for this kind of drinking. Nor has he figured out yet why he doesn't telephone his wife anymore to let her know he will be late on the pretext of "business reasons." He used to lie to her when he called, but at least he called. Now he doesn't even do that.

Then there was two weeks ago Friday. He and his wife went to a party. All their good friends were there. They get together a few times a year. And there is always plenty to drink. The fact that he had a few drinks before they went didn't particularly catch his attention, even though he had never done that before. And when, at the party, he went to get his second drink while the others were still on their first, that didn't particularly get his attention, even though this was something he had only started doing recently. What did have him shaken, though, is how "bombed" he actually got. Everyone, or almost everyone, drinks quite a bit at these parties. But this time he had so much that the others not only noticed it, they were both surprised and concerned. They had felt all evening that he was more with the drinking than with them and the party. His wife was embarrassed. She really didn't know what to say. He has tried to explain it not only to her, and maybe to the others, but also to himself. But deep down he is uneasy about the whole affair.

The explanation—the answer—for both these drinking episodes is very simple. This man has and will continue to experience loss of control over the amount that he drinks. There is the possibility that he will still have some drinking experiences with apparent control but he will inevitably and increasingly drink without control.

This kind of drinking problem has a name. It is alcoholism.

At this point I would suggest that even if you feel positive your drinking isn't alcoholism, don't skip over this part. Many people who think they know what alcoholism is know little about it. Many also hold very distorted and unhealthy ideas about alcoholism and the people who have it. In other words, this is a section that people who don't have alcoholism need to read just as much as people who do.

The thought of alcoholism as even a possibility may repel you, shock you, even come to you as an insult. Perhaps, like many others today, you may have heard or read enough about alcoholism to have found yourself wondering already whether that might be your problem. If you still see alcoholism as a dirty word, as a moral weakness, as an "unmanly" or "unwomanly" thing, keep on reading. Even if your drinking isn't alcoholism, what you read here may help change your understanding of alcoholism and attitudes toward alcoholics. Alcoholism is a word that describes an illness. Over 6,000,000 people have it. These millions and their families need all the understanding, acceptance, and hope our society can provide.

About one out of fourteen who drink end up with loss of control. It is no respecter of persons, economics or vocation. Only three to five percent of the over 6,000,000 people who have loss of control are on skid row. Most people with alcoholism are still in their homes and on their jobs. One out of four or five are women. (In some areas the percentage of women appears to be much higher.)

No one knows why some people lose control over alcohol. A significant number have never had control from the very beginning of their drinking. It is not uncommon for a man to think he has lost control only recently, but then when he thinks back on his drinking history to decide that inability to control the amount was present right from the start. The "why" of loss of control is still unknown but we do know that it is a reality.

Once loss of control is in the picture, it is there to stay. It is not only permanent; it is also progressive. There is no way to get rid of it—to get back to control. There are only two things that can happen to loss of control. It can get progressively worse or it can be arrested. In this sense it is like diabetes. This in a nutshell is alcoholism.

So we have drinking, drunkenness, problem drinking, and drinking problem (alcoholism). The first step is to help you decide which one of these describes your drinking. If your answer is either problem drinking or alcoholism, you must then determine which of these it is. Could that part of your drinking which you try unsuccessfully to explain to yourself—that part which really concerns you—be explained by loss of control? Fortunately there are ways to find out.

Maybe you only drink beer. Right at this point you may find yourself saying just that to yourself and dismissing the possibility of a drinking problem. Beware of that kind of reaction. The assumption that there can be no alcoholism with just beer drinking is not valid. A person who consumes a six-pack at home each night or a case on the weekend could well be evidencing loss of control. He appears to have more control than the fellow we have just described but it may be the same thing. The question is not "What do you drink?" but "Have you lost control?"

Possibly you are a person who does most of his drinking at home. Your wife may express concern about your drinking, but you don't see it as a problem. You go to work every day. But you are drinking a lot nearly every day following work and your weekends are essentially continuous drinking. This is quite a different kind of drinking than you did a few years back. You have had more than one experience that has embarrassed, if not shocked, your spouse and children, as well as yourself, but you have tried to pass those off. You may be viewing your drinking as your "right" or as something harmless that you just like to do. Without your knowing it, the kind of drinking you are now doing may be an evidence of the inability to drink within your own intention.

As alcoholism progresses there is increasing loss of control not only over the amount but also over the *time* when the alcoholic drinks. A man will not only repeat such episodes as missing dinner and making a fool of himself at a party when he didn't intend to; there will be an increase in frequency. No responsible person wants his drinking to interfere with his marriage, family, job, church or social responsibilities. And yet he will increasingly drink at times that interfere with any or all of these.

Here is a man who is drinking without control only on weekends or evenings. He is telling himself that his drinking is no problem. It is his business. But it is already interfering with his family responsibilities. Inevitably, however, his drinking will begin to interfere with his work. The time will come when he will be missing days because of drinking or when he will be drinking on the job. There are also the classic and tragic stories of those who, in their growing loss of control over the time when they drink, show up drunk or completely miss an extremely important meeting or appointment.

The point here is simply that if loss of control is present it will progress in terms of the time and number of times when the person will drink inappropriately.

But the real loss of control that many people, alcoholics and non-alcoholics alike, are unaware of is the inability to keep from taking the first drink all by oneself, relying completely upon one's own strength. Alcoholism is powerlessness over alcohol—total and complete.

This fact may appear to be utterly impossible. After all, if a man wants to stop drinking, all he has to do is make up his mind to stop and then stop. Absolutely true—unless alcoholism is present. The best a person who has alcoholism can do is delay the next drink. He can't, by himself, keep from eventually taking it.

One man said, "I didn't have a drink for four and a half years. I did that all by myself with help from no one." The reply to that statement was, "You didn't quit for four and a half years. You simply delayed taking your next drink for four and a half years." He went out to prove he was right—that this thing didn't have him, he had it—and in a much shorter period of time was drinking again without control.

When loss of control is present and a person tries to quit drinking all by himself, it is like putting the tea kettle on the stove with the burner turned on and plugging up the spout. Sooner or later something has to give. The alcoholic who tries it this way will be drinking again. The question isn't "if," it is "when" he will drink again. Thousands of alcoholics who have recovered by finding and accepting the help they needed, can look back and say, "I used to be so sure I could quit drinking if I really wanted to because I had done it so many times."

The truth is that when a person has alcoholism he has no way of knowing when he is going to drink, and when he drinks, he has no way of knowing when he is going to stop.

We have said that "loss of control" over alcohol is both permanent and progressive—that, like diabetes, it cannot be removed but only arrested. Because it is progressive, no one can be just a little bit alcoholic any more than a woman can be just a little bit pregnant. The only variable is where she is in the pregnancy. An alcoholic can be only months into loss of control, missing no work, with fairly minimal interference in the family, with no health problems because of drinking and yet just as much an alcoholic as a person at the end of the progression. The variable is not in the reality of alcoholism but in the stage of the progression.

There are many alcoholics in treatment situations who are being told these facts but really don't believe what they hear. But so certain is this information that the reality of it will surely, progressively, insidiously prove itself to the person who has loss of control. We who work with alcoholics know that if they don't come to believe it while they are in the treatment program, we or somebody else will someday see them again because of their drinking problem. The only difference will be that they will be further along in the progression.

What we are really emphasizing is that alcoholism is not only progressive, it is an illness. It is not a matter of failing to use or not using enough willpower. If willpower would or could do it, most alcoholics would have their sobriety because most have given that a real try. They have consistently failed after the most dedicated effort, always with the words, "This time I really mean it. I've had my last drink. I'm not going to drink again as long as I live."

If your drinking has gone into alcoholism, this "willpower" illusion will be one of the biggest hurdles to get over. To accept this not as being weak-willed but as having an illness is really the key. We will be referring to this again but mention it here because it is so basic in the understanding of alcoholism. Right now it could be very much at the forefront of your thinking. For now just remember this, if loss of control isn't in the picture, willpower will do it; if loss of control is in the picture, willpower won't do it.

To discover "loss of control" in one's drinking can be a real shock and hard on one's pride, but it can also be a source of relief because it provides an answer to the unanswered question, "Why do I continue to drink in a way that I neither intend or desire?" For that question "loss of control" removes the mystery.

If you are interested in finding out whether your drinking is evidence of "loss of control" over alcohol, or just problem drinking, keep on reading and you will be shown a way to find out for yourself. So this brings us to a significant juncture. Your drinking is now left squarely in your lap. That's where you want it and that's where we want it because that's where we both know it belongs.

2.

The
Acid
Test

One dictionary defines an acid test as "a severe and conclusive test to determine the genuineness" of something. There is an acid test for alcoholism. It is one you can give to yourself without the aid of anyone else. But your approach to it is all-important.

We would like to suggest a particular kind of attitude for you to adopt. First of all, keep in mind that we have said alcoholism is a disease, an illness, and that it is progressive. Now the important thing to do about any serious illness is to detect it as early as possible. In the case of cancer, there are usually some warning signals that indicate the possibility of its presence. A heavy smoker develops a different kind of cough, deeper and more persistent. A woman discovers a lump on her breast. Another person notices a mole becoming enlarged or occasional blood in the stool. Such symptoms prove nothing in themselves. But they may be signs of cancer.

What do you think you would do in such circumstances? What do you hope you would do? Those around you, of course, would hope you would see a doctor right away. There are diagnostic tests to determine whether malignancy exists. If it does, then early treatment can be effective. If it does not, you will be relieved of doubt and worry. But the important step is to take the test and find out, not to try to tell yourself you don't have cancer. If the disease is there, it won't disappear as a result of your attempts to forget it or to wish it away. Not only will it continue, it will grow progressively worse.

Hopefully, you will take the same sort of attitude toward your drinking. You may think you have found some possible danger signs of alcoholism. Of course early detection is not as critical as in cancer because alcoholics can fully recover even after the illness has been allowed to progress into later phases (as described in Chapter 3). But it gets no easier with time.

So even if you just can't believe that you could have alcoholism, we suggest that you allow for the possibility—if not because you are wondering about it, then because somebody else may be wondering about it. Usually the person who has alcoholism is the last one to recognize it. Consider taking the acid test. You don't have to see your doctor to do it. If it proves negative then you will feel relieved. If it proves positive, you can still keep on drinking as long as you want to. The only difference will be that now you will have good evidence that you have an illness and that sometime you will need to do something about it. You may decide you want to do something right now. Or you may decide you want to continue drinking for a while because you still get enough good effects from it for you to be willing to take whatever the consequences may be. But in that case it is important for you to know fully just what the consequences are if drinking is continued indefinitely.

When we talk about the acid test, we are not talking about "going on the water wagon." Many people who have a problem with their drinking attempt to deny or disprove its seriousness by simply stopping. The decision is made not to drink for a set period of time—a month, two months, during Lent, over the holidays—or to quit altogether, forever. This is an appealing idea. You may have thought about it or even tried it already, or your family or friends may have urged you to try it. But we are discouraging you from considering this kind of decision right now. The trouble is that such a test proves nothing and may be very misleading.

Consider the case of a person who has diabetes but doesn't know it. One day he hears about some possible symptoms and becomes concerned. He decides to cut down on his consumption of sugar. Possibly he convinces himself that he is beginning to feel better. But the fact is that he neither knows that he has the illness nor, if he does have it, has he taken adequate steps to arrest it. He needs first to find out for sure whether he has it, then to accept treatment that goes beyond avoiding sugar.

Similarly, a determination first has to be made whether alcoholism is present. If it is, the arresting of this disease involves something more than just putting the cap on the bottle for a while.

There is usually one big difference, however, between the victim of diabetes and the victim of alcoholism. You can be quite sure that the diabetic will accept the diagnosis of a doctor and follow the prescribed treatment. You cannot be so sure that the alcoholic will accept the diagnosis alcoholism and follow the treatment prescribed. *What this means is that not someone else, but the illness itself has to prove itself to the alcoholic.* The water wagon, the decision not to drink for a number of weeks, months or forever, doesn't allow for the illness, if it is present, proving itself to the person who has it. Such a decision only delays the illness from clearly revealing itself.

This leads to what may seem a startling statement: The only way for the illness of alcoholism to reveal and prove itself to the person who has it is for him to keep on drinking. The alcoholic wants to drink some more, whether he has been told he has alcoholism or has never heard the diagnosis. And if he wants to drink there is no value in somebody else telling him he can't. However, if the illness is present and proving itself to the person, then he will be more open to hear it say to him: "You no longer have your drinking. It has you."

The acid test involves your continuing to drink. It allows you to find out first of all if you even have to think about quitting drinking. If you haven't lost control you don't have to quit unless you want to. And if you want to you can. But if you have lost control, you have to begin to think about finding a way to quit your drinking—that is, if you want to save your job, your family, your life itself. And, if you have lost control and decide you want to quit, then you will have to discover that even though you want to quit, you can't do it by yourself.

14

You need outside help.

Some try this test with an air of bravado, telling themselves they are sure they will pass it. Others have a more cautious attitude, feeling somewhat uncertain but hoping that they will be able to make it. However you may feel at this point, we will be frank in saying that if you really don't yet want to know one way or the other, don't try this test. It is that good.

If you decide to take the test, and if you are married, talk it over with your wife. Have her read this section—particularly if she is pushing to have you stop drinking altogether right now. She may be surprised that someone is suggesting that you get involved in a procedure that necessitates the continuation of drinking. Chances are, though, that this will make sense to her, too, and that she, with you, will be willing to have a "let's really find out" attitude. Both of you should adopt a wait-and-see approach to the acid test.

It is important that you not try to make a "big deal" out of the test. Don't announce it to your friends. You are not out to disprove that you are a weakling who is incapable of handling his drinking. Don't see this as a contest with your spouse to show that you are right and she is wrong. You are not out to prove anything to anybody else. You are simply involved in a testing procedure to find out if you have a disease—alcoholism—that millions have, a treatable disease for which the chances of recovery are very good. Let's return to the diabetic: If there were some question whether you might have diabetes, you would take the necessary test not to prove you didn't have it, but rather to find out whether you have it or not.

Such an "experiment" must include the understanding that if loss of control is demonstrated, you will be willing to expose yourself to the kind of help that is indicated, even if you still don't really believe you need it. In other words, it is agreed that everyone concerned—including you—is ready at least to begin to take alcoholism seriously if it is present, and to talk with someone about it.

The first step in the test is for you to decide what you consider is reasonable, desirable, appropriate drinking, as far as you are concerned. Make the determination in terms of number of drinks and in terms of ounces of alcohol. One drink is to be thought of as one ounce of distilled spirits, one bottle of beer, one glass of wine. Set what you consider a reasonable limit of drinks for you for any given day— two, three, four, five, six. What do you—not somebody else, but *you* —think is a reasonable amount?

Once you have set your own limit, make a firm commitment not to exceed this amount. This does not mean that you must or will drink up to your limit every day, but it does mean that on *any* day when you do drink, you won't drink more than the number you have decided is reasonable. Note the word *any*: that includes birthdays, weddings, holidays, parties or celebrations of any sort.

Now you are going to give yourself an opportunity to see if you can drink with control within the limits you have set, never going beyond that limit on any day for any reason. The period of time is three months. Some experts say six months is better, but three is adequate in most cases.

If and when you drink beyond your intention, beyond the limit you have set for any given day during this three month period, then you agree with yourself to reflect seriously about possible explanations—other than loss of control. You may, for instance, feel that you were doing very well, but that on this one occasion you just didn't try hard enough. Or you may feel that you tried too hard and got too anxious about the whole thing. Or you may decide that some unexpected set-back or upheaval took place on the job, in your marriage, or whatever, and that you just decided for the moment "what the hell" and forgot about the test. Whatever explanation you may provide after some reflection, the fact of the matter will be that the possibility of loss of control will be much less of a question mark at that time. Remember the daily limit is set for three months and this limit is not to be exceeded for any reason.

Whatever possible explanation you may come up with for exceeding the limit once, start again on a new three month cycle. The next excessive drinking episode, if there is a next one, will be firm evidence of loss of control. It will then be the only possible explanation. You may still not be convinced. But you should know that your denial runs up against the experience of countless men and women with drinking problems. This fact alone hopefully will prompt you to consult someone you trust who knows something about alcoholism.

Should loss of control be established, you need to remember that this does not make you some kind of freak or moral weakling, a person essentially different from other people. It simply means that you are one out of every thirteen or fourteen people whose drinking has gone into alcoholism. In fact, people who have this disease and begin on the road that leads to recovery discover that they are in some illustrious company.

No matter who or how many people may feel you have a drinking problem, the primary consideration is whether you really believe it. If you don't think that it is even a possibility, then you obviously won't be doing much about it. The fact that you have read this far could well mean that you have enough concern about your drinking to consider seriously taking the test to establish if loss of control is present.

There is the possibility that having read about the "acid test" you are already convinced that you can't pass that. If so, just continue reading. Hopefully you will find the rest of this book helpful in enlarging your understanding of alcoholism and the essentials for sobriety.

While you are making up your mind about the "acid test," here is another test to help determine whether your drinking has gone into alcoholism. These questions were developed by Johns Hopkins University Hospital for deciding whether a patient is an alcoholic. Answer each question as honestly as you can. If you want to, you can have your spouse check to see how she (or he) would answer these twenty questions in regard to your drinking.

Are You An Alcoholic?

Do you lose time from work due to drinking?
Is drinking making your home life unhappy?
Do you drink because you are shy with other people?

17

Is drinking affecting your reputation?

Have you ever felt remorse after drinking?

Have you gotten into financial difficulties as a result of drinking?

Do you turn to lower companions and an inferior environment when drinking?

Does your drinking make you careless of your family's welfare?

Has your ambition decreased since drinking?

Do you crave a drink at a definite time daily?

Do you want a drink the next morning?

Does drinking cause you to have difficulty in sleeping?

Has your efficiency decreased since drinking?

Is drinking jeopardizing your job or business?

Do you drink to escape from worries or trouble?

Do you drink alone?

Have you ever had a complete loss of memory as a result of drinking?

Has your physician ever treated you for drinking?

Do you drink to build up your self-confidence?

Have you ever been to a hospital or institution on account of drinking?

Three "yes" answers may well mean alcoholism. If there are four "yes" answers, alcoholism is almost certain to be present.

There are many other signs that indicate whether a serious drinking problem exists. The reports of people who have gone through the experience of alcohol addiction have given us a large body of facts about the illness. We are now able to describe the development of the disease in terms of progressive symptoms and stages.

3.

The

Progressive

Symptoms

If your efforts at controlled drinking fail, then it is especially important that you be aware of the progressive nature and symptoms of alcoholism. The progression is inevitable. Alcoholism never just levels off and stays at one point, nor does it ever subside, reverse itself and get better. Inevitably, insidiously the spiral is downward. What you will notice in the progression is not only that the drinking grows worse and resulting problems increase, but that more and more of the person's life is taken from him, physically, emotionally, socially, vocationally, spiritually. The personal loss and isolation continuously intensify. All of this is not determined on the basis of who the person is and what strengths he may or may not have. Rather it is determined by the inevitabilities of the disease itself, just like the inevitabilities of cancer, no matter who the person is who has the disease.

If a person who has lost control doesn't believe the progression downward will happen to him, time will prove that the disease is no respecter of the persons who have it. As you read about these progressive symptoms, remember our reference to a woman being pregnant. She cannot be a little bit pregnant. The only difference is where she may be in the progression of her pregnancy. This we underscore again because if you come across symptoms you haven't experienced yet, you may think they could never be reality for you. The fact is that most of them will in time appear if the disease isn't arrested and the uncontrolled drinking continues.

The only exception to this is that not all the progressive symptoms will inevitably appear in each case of alcoholism, nor will those that do appear always come along in the same order. However, what is inevitable is the general cluster of symptoms. At a given point you may not have one or two of them but you will have the general condition described by the various symptoms.

Indicating Signs

First of all there are the "indicating signs" of alcoholism. Any more than the first three or four signs may already point to early alcoholism. Some drinkers with a number of these signs may become concerned about the change in their drinking and modify their drinking habits. Frequently, however, the drinker does not allow himself to notice serious basic changes in his drinking and feels simply that he is having "more fun, more often." What he fails to see is that in order to have more fun more often he needs more anesthesia—more alcohol—more often. The signs pointing to basic changes may include any of the following:

1. More frequent drinking episodes.
2. More drinking during these episodes—drinking more heavily, more often.
3. Drinking to relieve tension.
4. Increase in alcohol tolerance.
5. Sneaking drinks.
6. Desire to continue when others stop.
7. Uneasiness in situations where there is no alcohol.
8. Relief drinking commences.
9. Gulping drinks.
10. Possible memory lapses (blackouts) after heavy drinking.
11. Preoccupation with drinking.
12. Secret irritation when drinking is discussed, and feelings of self-justification.
13. Getting drunk begins to be a regular phenomenon.

vill discuss just a few of these signs. Sneaking drinks may mean alcoholism is already present. It is an obvious indication that a person wants more than others are drinking and that he feels guilty or uncomfortable about it. If we do anything in a sneaky fashion we are feeling guilty about what we are doing. A person who sneaks drinks is giving clear indication that his primary interest is not social drinking but taking sedation. There are all kinds of ways to do this, such as serving oneself doubles while giving others singles, taking one or two extra while mixing drinks for others, having drinks before going to a party, or hiding bottles.

If and when he experiences a blackout, a drinker will be frightened. He may not talk about it. If he can't remember the next day some things that happened at a party he may joke about how much he drank. But if he can't remember driving the car home and into the garage, he may with great fear examine the fender for dents or blood. The blackout is not passing out, it is drawing a blank while one is doing whatever one is doing. It cannot be recognized by others because the person in the blackout is apparently functioning quite well.

A blackout by itself may have little or no significance in terms of alcoholism being present, but it is never to be eliminated as a possible danger signal. Anyone who has had more than one blackout ought to give very serious consideration to what may be in store for him as far as alcoholism is concerned. More than one blackout is sufficient reason to question one's control.

Often a drinker develops a preoccupation with alcohol. He constantly associates alcohol with "feeling good" or "having a good time." At his work he finds himself thinking about and waiting for his next drink. Drinks at noon, or on the way home, or just as soon as he gets home may become basic in his thoughts. If he is going to a party or any other activity he wants to know whether there will be alcohol. If not, he may or may not attend; if he does go he won't really be interested or enjoy himself. He will be thinking about drinking.

It is not surprising that gulping drinks comes into the picture. If the factor of sedation rather than just social drinking is primary, gulping is the quickest way to get the desired effect. He becomes "the man with the empty glass."

There is also the periodic alcoholic whose pattern for drinking is quite different. He is either totally abstinent or drinking every day. There may be prolonged periods of abstinence, but once he starts drinking, that is all he does. His family and job are completely neglected, and he continues to drink until he runs out of money, gets into serious trouble, or becomes so sick that he can't continue. As the alcoholism progresses, his periods of drinking will increase in frequency.

Guilt about drinking is initially an occasional and passing experience following certain times of drinking that are excessive according to his own judgment. Feeling guilty, he grows more and more sensitive. So he experiences irritation when drinking is discussed. He not only feels guilty about his drinking, but may fear that conversation about drinking may lead to conversation about *his* drinking.

Any person with a number of the "indicating signs" may already have left one road and turned down another marked Alcoholism. At very least these features suggest problem drinking. There is need for help in dealing with the problems being expressed through alcohol. It would be a good idea to talk with some knowledgeable person about it. A counselor at this point may uncover several possibilities:

1) Problems for which the person needs help together with the need to modify drinking habits and patterns.
2) The advisability of quitting drinking altogether because the vulnerability for alcoholism involves too great a risk.
3) Determination, through the acid test or other means, of the presence of alcoholism and the need for direct treatment of the disease.

The major difficulty here is that many people who have a number of the indicating signs do not seriously look at their drinking soon enough and, if indicated, seek outside help for their problems. They continue with their drinking and progress into alcoholism.

We will divide the progression of alcoholism into three phases: Early, Middle, and Late. If the "acid test" has established the fact of loss of control, then the drinking problem is at least in the early phase of alcoholism, if not further. And unless you are one of those who happened to have loss of control from the time of your first drinking experiences, you may already have identified a number of the "indicating signs" in the earlier progression of your drinking problem.

Early Alcoholism Phase

Loss of control is itself progressive in the advance of alcoholism. It involves a growing inability to drink within one's own intention in terms of amount, time, and place. Sooner or later comes loss of control over the ability to quit drinking altogether without outside help. If a person has lost control over the amount he drinks, he very likely has already lost control over the ability to quit on his own without feeling considerable discomfort in his abstinence.

Whenever we are personally involved in behavior that we want to perceive as being different than it really is, we try to explain it away. The alcoholic begins to develop what will quickly become an elaborate rationalization and alibi system. The emphasis is on "elaborate system." He provides all kinds of reasons for why he drinks the way he does. With this comes lying about his drinking. He does this partly to answer family and friends, but even more to reassure himself and avoid the obvious reality of loss of control. Underneath this elaborate rationalization and alibi system he harbors the idea that somehow, someday he will be able to control and enjoy his drinking. This is the great obsession of every alcoholic. He is unaware of the fact that he is no longer capable of either having or enjoying controlled drinking. Lying about his drinking becomes "par for the course," and there is an increasing frequency of relief drinking.

He now feels guilt not just because of drinking too much, but also because his drinking is different in quality from that of family members and friends. The amount he drinks has changed but so has the reason why he drinks, without his knowing it. He is in a way already drinking alone even while he is drinking together with his friends.

Attempts by family members to discuss the problem with him result in failure. He may minimize or deny his drinking problem or even refuse to talk about it. By now he has developed a good repertoire of rationalizations which prevent productive discussion. There may also be the feeling that if his spouse would just "get off his back" about the drinking, he wouldn't drink so much.

Incidence of memory blackouts may increase. This may frighten him a little more and he may handle that by telling himself he has to watch it. Or he may just try to dismiss it as something that has no great significance.

Middle Alcoholism Phase

As the results of drinking become more apparent, social pressures begin to increase from spouse, friends, employer and others. This is painful and he seeks to handle it by strengthening his rationalization system. He tells himself that they don't understand, that they are making too much of his drinking, that *they* are the problem, not he. Unfortunately, most of the people around him may at this point see his problem as weakness rather than loss of control due to an illness. Promises and resolutions and efforts to control fail repeatedly. These come into the picture usually because of pressure from the spouse or another family member. But he never succeeds.

He may begin to show grandiose and aggressive behavior. He's the big wheel, the big spender, the guy who is in command. Some of this he may even express with people he doesn't know, ordering drinks for everyone at the bar.

He may then go on the water wagon to prove to himself, and maybe also to others, that he really doesn't have a problem, can take it or leave it and if necessary quit on his own. A period of time is usually set—a month, three months, six months. If he makes it through this period he feels he has proved he can leave it alone and then proceeds to drink without control again. If he does not make it through the time set for abstinence he always has a good reason (excuse) for why he didn't. The fact that going on the wagon never enters the mind of someone who doesn't have a drinking problem is completely overlooked. It is interesting to note here, that although the problem is loss of control, for many drinkers the possibility of trying to control the drinking rather than go on the water wagon is not considered.

Sometimes the drinker begins to perceive the problem in terms of when or what he drinks. He will try to change his patterns of drinking behavior. This too is really an attempt to break the hold alcohol has on him. He decides perhaps to stay away from distilled spirits and stick to beer. No longer is he going to drink alone or during the week or stop for a couple of drinks after work. As these measures fail it only becomes more apparent that the problem isn't what, where, or with whom, but simply loss of control.

To experience change in his family and social relationships is hard on his self-esteem. Family closeness really begins to deteriorate. Friends begin to avoid him, and he begins to avoid them. This he may try to handle by excessive criticism of them. He seeks out new friends with whom to drink, that is, people whose drinking patterns and behavior more closely harmonize with his own. He fails to see that the new acquaintances, his "real friends," are only drinking companions and nothing more.

Then comes a significant change in his internal feelings—persistent remorse and guilt. He can't dismiss the guilt feelings and there is a lingering kind of oppressive remorse over what he is doing to himself and others. He himself becomes his severest judge, but self-condemnation merely multiplies the guilt feelings, from which the only escape is drinking. So he relieves a problem caused by drinking with more persistent drinking. The downward spiral picks up steam: drinking, guilt, more drinking, greater guilt. . . .

By now he may have quit a job or two because he realized it was in jeopardy because of his drinking. Or he may have lost a job. If he quit before he was fired, he will tell himself that he never lost a job because of drinking, which to him means that it isn't a serious problem.

You will remember that we mentioned the progressive loss of life itself. Drinking becomes of central importance. Whereas he previously didn't want it interfering with his primary responsibilities and interests, now it has become the main thing, the essence of his life. He is captive to alcohol. There is a narrowing of his range of interests. Life is being reduced to himself and the bottle. There is severe neglect of his wife and children and job. Last year he went on the annual fishing trip but was drunk all the time. This year he didn't go at all because of drinking. For a while he kept going to church or his club because he had once been active, but now he goes rarely or never.

Soon comes the persistent feeling of marked self-pity. A whole new array of reasons are given other than his drinking for the absence of old friends and the presence of new drinking companions as well as the problems he is having in his marriage. Nobody cares and everyone is against him—"poor me."

The idea may strike him that the problem is where he is living, or the kind of job he has, or the in-laws. He seeks to solve everything through geographic escape. But no matter where he is or what he is doing or how far away he moves from certain people, his drinking troubles continue.

The family realizes that they have to plan their life apart from him. So there is the need to change family activities. They can't count on him. The spouse may seriously begin thinking about separation.

As he begins to dislike, actually to hate, himself more and more, and is filled with self-pity, he will evidence unreasonable resentment towards others. Without consciously realizing it, he is hoping that those to whom he directs his resentments will feel guilty and respond in a way that shows they feel they are responsible for his problem.

There develops such a desperation about drinking that he has to begin to protect his supply. He must make sure there is always enough and that nobody removes or destroys his liquor. He cleverly seeks hiding places. Sometimes he has the dilemma of having forgotten where he hid his supply, like the man in *Days of Wine and Roses*.

Drinking becomes so paramount that there is neglect of nutrition and the beginning of some real physical complications. As drinking intensifies, appetite for food declines. Besides, food interferes with the maximum effect of the alcohol. He drinks and doesn't eat. Although appearing well nourished, he may be suffering from malnutrition.

Late Alcoholism Phase

In time the alcoholic will inevitably go through the experience of having to be hospitalized for his drinking. When released he is apt to feel like a new man and to find himself saying "never again." Unless he has learned about alcoholism and started treatment, his resolve is soon forgotten.

When he reaches regular morning drinking then he is really on the merry-go-round and entering the late alcoholism phase. Drink has become a constant need that knows no time or place.

Isolated completely by and with his drinking, he now may start going on binges and benders, drinking for days at a time. Socially he has now deteriorated to a point at which he completely cuts himself off from family, friends, and society. There is growing disregard for everyone and everything. If necessary he will lie, cheat, even steal to get more liquor. If he has funds to support this kind of drinking he may continue to live with the delusion that he really has no problem. But the drinking increasingly leaves him shaken, frightened, guilt-ridden.

Self-deception and lying about drinking are sooner or later followed by a more complete life-encompassing ethical deterioration. Instead of just lying about his drinking he becomes a lying person. He may begin to use friends to preserve his drinking or get him out of jams that resulted because of his drinking. His child may have a savings fund or paper route money at home which the alcoholic may find himself stealing for drinks. If he has been active in his religious life, he completely drops that. There may well be cheating on work time and even putting his hand into the company till. All these actions are a serious violation of his own basic principles. The only remedy for his guilt is more alcohol.

He will begin to show signs of deterioration in his thinking. Family and friends may begin to wonder if he has become mentally ill. Temporary alcoholic psychosis, such as delirium tremens, may appear. The possibility of brain damage and psychosis now begins to loom.

Unless finances allow for sustaining his economic level, he is now heading in the direction of a skid row existence. Perhaps he has already lost his family and a number of jobs. Even if he still has financial resources he is taking on the pattern of skid row drinking: expensive hospitals substitute for flophouses and jails.

Whereas his capacity for alcohol once was very high—he could "drink anyone under the table"—there has been a progressive loss of tolerance and now it is very low. Consequently there may be a decrease in amounts consumed. He becomes disabled much more rapidly.

One of the most anxiety-producing realities is the onset of indefinable fears, gnawing at him with a sense of terrible impending doom and destruction. Life can no longer be faced without alcohol. The only relief for the terrible results of his drinking progression is more drinking—persistent, compulsive drinking. Drinking now becomes an obsession as well as a compulsion. He is living to drink and drinking to live. The only possible relief is oblivion.

As we look at these symptoms in the downward progression, it is apparent that alcoholism gradually envelops the whole person. There is an insidious deterioration intellectually, physically, emotionally, socially and spiritually. Life itself is slowly but surely stripped away. The difficult obstacle in all of this is the elaborate rationalization system, and again we emphasize the word system, that prevents the alcoholic from allowing himself to see and feel the obvious life-removing progression. Not until that system collapses can there be any real hope and help for the alcoholic.

As you reflect on this progression and seek to determine whether any of it describes your own experience and, if so, where you might be, it is important for you to be aware of the fact that many alcoholics are recovering while they are in the middle phase. The key question is how soon the person will both recognize and accept the fact that he does have alcoholism—a progressive disease for which he needs outside help.

4.

The

Turning

Point

Many people who have alcoholism take some steps toward seeking help before they are really ready to accept the kind of help they need. Sometimes this happens because the alcoholic's spouse is insisting that something has to be done, sometimes because the boss is saying so, sometimes because he has received a drunken driving charge and the judge told him to. Seldom are the first steps toward help taken purely because of personal desire and initiative. Usually there is pressure being brought to bear from an outside source. If the attitudes are nonmoralistic and the pressure is applied firmly, these pressures can be helpful. The main thing is that the person who has or may have a drinking problem begins to see someone who knows something about this illness.

Perhaps you have already talked to someone—your pastor, the counselor at the local Council on Alcoholism, your physician, a friend. From this book and possibly from other contacts you have already learned something about alcoholism. The vital need is to maintain some kind of contact with someone whom you can trust who also knows about alcoholism. The reason for this is that usually it takes time to reach the point where you really are ready to accept your alcoholism and actively involve yourself in the help you need. By being in touch with someone who understands the illness, you may still continue to drink, but such a contact may also hasten the day when you will want help to keep from drinking.

If alcoholism is in the picture, the real turning point is the complete collapse of the rationalization system and the acceptance, without reservation, that you are an alcoholic. This is called the surrender phenomenon—the readiness and capacity to give in and stop fighting the obvious and irreversible fact of loss of control. It is to accept powerlessness over alcohol and to acknowledge the reality of a life that is becoming or has become unmanageable because of this fact.

For most people with a problem for which they need help, intellectual awareness precedes gut-level acceptance. Sometimes it takes awhile for such understanding to seep down from the head into the insides. And we know that any understanding we have is not really a part of us until it gets accepted deep inside of ourselves. A psychiatrist, now deceased, Dr. Harry Tiebout, has described the difference by using the words compliance and surrender. Compliance is knowing alcoholism is present but still wishing it weren't. Compliance is knowing it intellectually but still believing deep inside it just can't be so: alcohol cannot have me licked—it doesn't make sense that I can't handle my drinking. Compliance is like the man who has lost his leg, but hasn't accepted the reality of it. He knows the leg is gone. He knows he is going to have to live without it. He has mentally resigned himself to the unavoidable reality but deep inside he hasn't yet accepted it. He continues to wish it weren't so, wonders why it had to happen to him, wants what cannot be, feels sorry for himself.

Sometimes compliance looks very much like real acceptance or surrender. A young man in his middle thirties had just been on a severe drinking episode. He knew he had lost a good job because of it. He wasn't sure if his marriage would continue. He was feeling all kinds of pain—physical ache, guilt, remorse, self-hatred, loneliness, fear, a sense of impending doom, hopelessness. The reality of the seriousness of his drinking problem was breaking through to him as it never had before. At the moment there was no way to duck it except to seek oblivion through more drinking. But he was too sick and frightened to do that. All of this was expressed in these words: "I thought I could lick this thing, but it's got me licked. I need help."

That sounded as though he was really ready for help. When he learned that there was a place he might be able to go for treatment, he was much relieved. After a call was made and it was learned that a bed was available he was even more relieved and expressed great appreciation. Three days after entering the treatment facility, feeling better physically, he left the unit, walked into the office where he had entered as a trembling frightened man and remarked, "I think I can handle it." In the midst of his distress he had complied with the reality of powerlessness over alcohol. When his well-being was restored, it became clear that his surrender was in reality compliance.

Surrender is that phenomenon, or the beginning of that phenomenon, in which the whole person—intellectually and deep inside—is ready and able to say yes to loss of control, without reservation and with the desire to accept the help needed to keep from drinking. With compliance an alcoholic may stay sober for awhile—sometimes for quite awhile—as he conforms with what he is told to do. With surrender sobriety endures because acceptance of the reality of alcoholism brings into being a basic change in attitude and sense of responsibility—without which sobriety is a grim business.

There is a prayer that many people recovering from alcoholism regularly use. "God grant me the serenity to accept things I cannot change, courage to change things I can, and wisdom to know the difference." To achieve this kind of serenity, courage, and wisdom doesn't come easily to most people. But without it there can be no real recovery.

What is frequently involved in the process is this: By having some contact with a knowledgeable and understanding person and by doing some reading, your drinking begins to get spoiled. Some of the fun—if there is still any fun in it—gets taken away because now you know you are not just drinking but have a drinking problem; you initiate some attempts at control or try some self-help procedure to quit drinking; your drinking continues to be a problem or—if you are trying to leave it alone—you find yourself quite tense, irritable, and unhappy in the process. If any of this has been a part of your experience it may be helpful to know that it is par for the course.

You may also have another experience. If you are in contact with a

THE PROGRESSIVE **DISEASE of ALCOHO**
(READ FROM LEFT...DOW

ADDICTION

HEAVY SOCIAL DRINKING - 5 OR MORE PER OCCASION

2 TO 25 YEARS

- INCREASE IN ALCOHOL TOLERANCE — DRINKING TO RELIEVE TENSION
- DESIRE TO CONTINUE WHEN OTHERS STOP — DRINKING BEFORE A DRINKING FUNCTION
- RELIEF DRINKING COMMENCES — UNCOMFORTABLE IN SITUATION WHERE THERE IS NO ALCOHOL
- PREOCCUPATION WITH ALCOHOL (THINKING ABOUT NEXT DRINK) — OCCASIONAL MEMORY LAPSES AFTER HEAVY DRINKING
- SECRET IRRITATION WHEN YOUR DRINKING IS DISCUSSED

LOSS OF CONTROL PHASE - RATIONALIZATION BEGINS

- LYING ABOUT DRINKING TO EVERYBODY (RATIONALIZATION)
- INCREASING FREQUENCY OF RELIEF DRINKING

EARLY

- SNEAKING DRINKS
- DRINKING BOLSTERED WITH EXCUSES — URGENCY OF FIRST DRINK
- INCREASED MEMORY BLACKOUTS — INCREASING DEPENDENCE ON ALCOHOL
- TREMORS AND EARLY MORNING DRINKS — FEELING OF GUILT ABOUT DRINKING
- COMPLETE DISHONESTY — UNABLE TO DISCUSS PROBLEMS
- LOSS OF OTHER INTERESTS — PROMISES AND RESOLUTIONS FAIL
- EFFORTS TO CONTROL FAIL REPEATEDLY — GRANDIOSE AND AGGRESSIVE B
- FAMILY AND FRIENDS AVOIDED — FAMILY, WORK AND MONEY PR
- NEGLECT OF FOOD

12 TO 15 YRS AVERAGE

MIDDLE — **LOSS OF JOB** → — DRINKING ALONE - SECRE

RADICAL DETERIORATION OF FAMILY RELATIONSHIPS

NOW THINKS: "ACTIVIT INTERFERE WITH MY D

2 TO 10 YEARS

- PHYSICAL DETERIORATION — UNREASONABLE RES
- MORAL DETERIORATION — "WATER WAGON" ATT
- URGENT NEED FOR MORNING DRINK — LOSS OF WILL POW
- SANITARIUM OR HOSPITAL — ONSET OF LENGTH
- PERSISTENT REMORSE — GEOGRAPHICAL E
- LOSS OF FAMILY — IMPAIRED THIN
- DECREASE IN ALCOHOLIC TOLERANCE — DRINKING WIT
- HOSPITAL / SANITARIUM — SUCCESSIVE LE
- UNABLE TO INITIATE ACTION — INDEFINABLE
- OBSESSION WITH DRINKING — UNABLE TO W
- ALL ALIBIS EXHAUSTED

5 TO 7 YRS AVERAGE

LATE

COMPLETE ABANDONMENT

DISTRIBUTED BY
ALCOHOLISM COUNCIL OF
GREATER LOS ANGELES
1290 WILSHIRE BLVD.
LOS ANGELES, CALIFORNIA

DERELICTION
DRINKING AWAY
"SYMPTOMS OF DRINKING"
IN VICIOUS CIRCLES

THE OF A

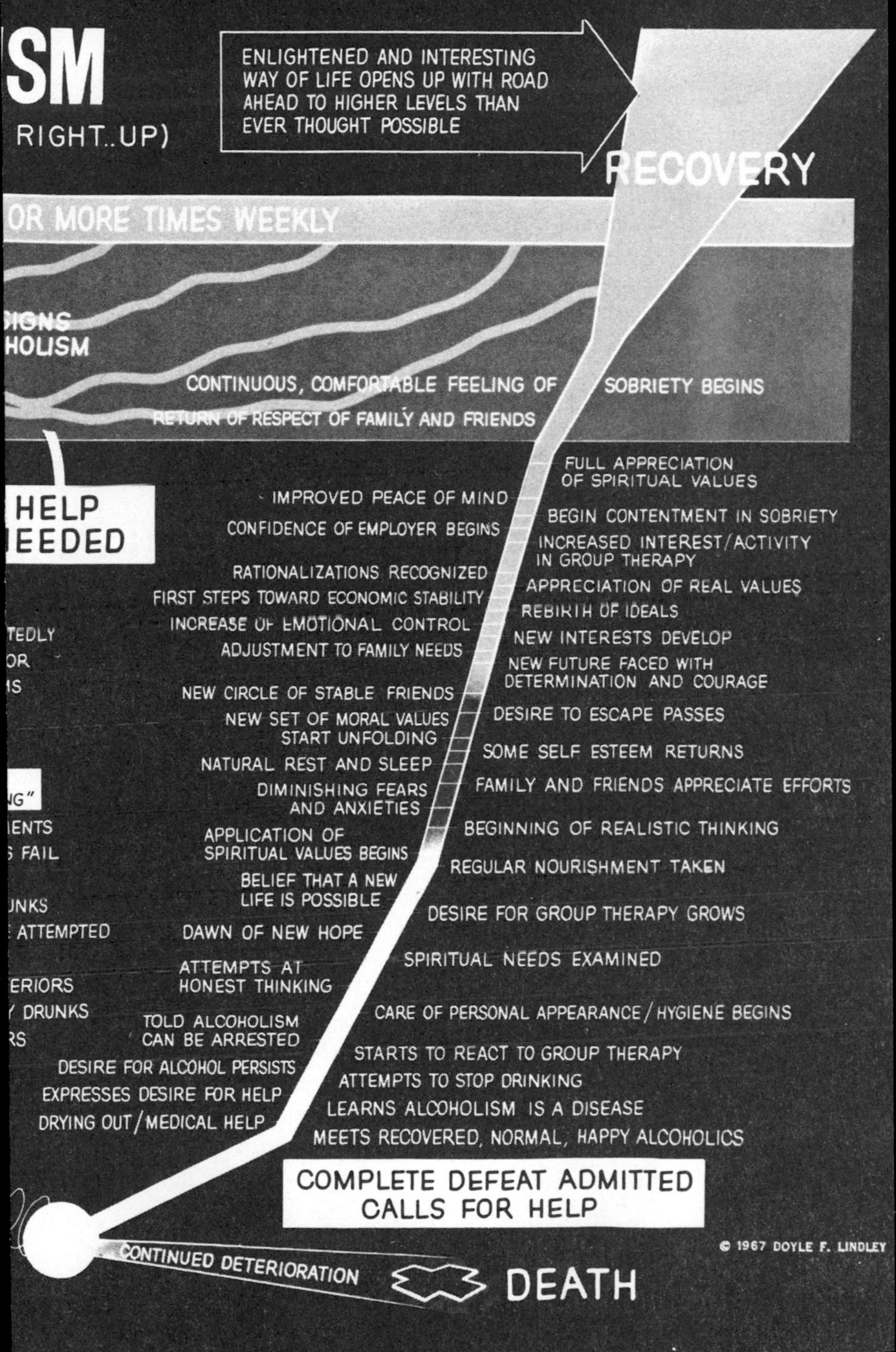

SM
RIGHT..UP)
ENLIGHTENED AND INTERESTING WAY OF LIFE OPENS UP WITH ROAD AHEAD TO HIGHER LEVELS THAN EVER THOUGHT POSSIBLE
RECOVERY
OR MORE TIMES WEEKLY
HOLISM
CONTINUOUS, COMFORTABLE FEELING OF
SOBRIETY BEGINS
RETURN OF RESPECT OF FAMILY AND FRIENDS
HELP
EEDED
FULL APPRECIATION OF SPIRITUAL VALUES
IMPROVED PEACE OF MIND
BEGIN CONTENTMENT IN SOBRIETY
CONFIDENCE OF EMPLOYER BEGINS
INCREASED INTEREST/ACTIVITY IN GROUP THERAPY
RATIONALIZATIONS RECOGNIZED
APPRECIATION OF REAL VALUES
FIRST STEPS TOWARD ECONOMIC STABILITY
REBIRTH OF IDEALS
INCREASE OF EMOTIONAL CONTROL
NEW INTERESTS DEVELOP
TEDLY
ADJUSTMENT TO FAMILY NEEDS
NEW FUTURE FACED WITH DETERMINATION AND COURAGE
NEW CIRCLE OF STABLE FRIENDS
DESIRE TO ESCAPE PASSES
NEW SET OF MORAL VALUES START UNFOLDING
SOME SELF ESTEEM RETURNS
NATURAL REST AND SLEEP
DIMINISHING FEARS AND ANXIETIES
FAMILY AND FRIENDS APPRECIATE EFFORTS
IENTS
FAIL
APPLICATION OF SPIRITUAL VALUES BEGINS
BEGINNING OF REALISTIC THINKING
REGULAR NOURISHMENT TAKEN
BELIEF THAT A NEW LIFE IS POSSIBLE
UNKS
DESIRE FOR GROUP THERAPY GROWS
ATTEMPTED
DAWN OF NEW HOPE
SPIRITUAL NEEDS EXAMINED
ERIORS
ATTEMPTS AT HONEST THINKING
DRUNKS
CARE OF PERSONAL APPEARANCE/HYGIENE BEGINS
TOLD ALCOHOLISM CAN BE ARRESTED
STARTS TO REACT TO GROUP THERAPY
DESIRE FOR ALCOHOL PERSISTS
ATTEMPTS TO STOP DRINKING
EXPRESSES DESIRE FOR HELP
LEARNS ALCOHOLISM IS A DISEASE
DRYING OUT/MEDICAL HELP
MEETS RECOVERED, NORMAL, HAPPY ALCOHOLICS
COMPLETE DEFEAT ADMITTED CALLS FOR HELP
CONTINUED DETERIORATION
DEATH
© 1967 DOYLE F. LINDLEY

knowledgeable and understanding person who in various ways spoils your drinking, for some strange reason you may find yourself continuing to have appointments with him rather than avoiding him. If that happens—even though it may baffle you—remember it is good. It usually means something positive is in your relationship with him.

Sometimes the person with alcoholism becomes immediately ready for help. Things begin to fall into place. What he hears makes sense. He wonders why he hasn't heard it sooner. Acceptance is an immediate reality. He is at the turning point and turns. He sets foot on the road to sobriety and that will be the beginning of the end of his drinking. You may be one of the fortunate ones who experiences surrender right away. But chances are better that you will go through a period and a process in which a part of you starts saying yes to the reality of alcoholism, while another part of you deep inside continues to say no. If alcoholism is present, you will know on some level that you do have it. You will become slowly but increasingly aware of your need for help to free you from the clutches of the illness, but very likely there will be a part of you strongly resisting the whole business. That is a rough spot to be in but usually an unavoidable one along the way that eventually leads to recovery. Once you seriously begin to seek sobriety, you may do well for awhile and then have some trouble again. A relapse, even though it isn't necessary in recovery, is not uncommonly the experience that finally sinks the reality of alcoholism deep inside.

Surrender comes to individuals in different ways and at different times along the progressive road of alcoholism. To some it comes early, to some late, to some it comes only after they have lost everything and to some, unfortunately, it never comes at all. If you have alcoholism and if what you have been reading so far makes any kind of sense to you, your chances of coming to the turning point should be very good. Although you can't make yourself surrender, once you reach the point where you really want sobriety, it will come. The main thing is that you are aware of the fact that there is good reason for you to be hopeful of recovery because there is help—once you are ready for it. One clue as to what may or may not be happening in terms of surrender is your reservations and qualifications. Listen to how you are thinking and to what you are saying to yourself and others. If you find a frequency of "should," "maybe," "perhaps," "ought to" in regard to your drinking problem and getting help, then you know you aren't yet at the turning point. When you hear yourself say, "I know" and "I want" in response to your problem and the help that you need, and you really mean it, then you could well be at the turning point.

If you are an alcoholic you have already experienced something of the downward progression of the illness. When you come to the turning point and set foot on the road to recovery, a lot more is in store for you than just putting the cork on the bottle. Alcoholism becomes a way of life. Now you have an opportunity to get involved in another way of life that will make possible a whole new set of feelings and values. Feelings that feel good. Values that give you two of the things you want most—your own self-respect and peace of mind. Imagine what it will feel like to be able to look in the mirror and like the person you see. Alcoholics tell us that self-respect is one of the treasured rewards of recovery. (D. A. Stewart has written a book about alcoholism entitled *Thirst for Freedom* [Center City, Minn.: Hazeldon, 1960].) When you reach the turning point you arrive at the moment when that thirst can be satisfied. Besides the freedom not to drink, there lies ahead freedom from the guilt, the lying, the fear, the loneliness,—freedom to live soberly, responsibly and meaningfully. It may seem now that such freedom is "way off there someplace" but you should know that it can be a reality in your recovery. Such freedom, peace of mind and self-respect will probably not come immediately in one full bundle but gradually, and surely in due time.

You may be interested at this point in looking again at the chart (page 32) that shows not only the downward progression of alcoholism but also the upward progression of sobriety. Too many people are only aware of the negative aspects of alcoholism that precede the positive fulfillments in recovery. On the right hand side of this chart you will notice that although stopping drinking is the immediate and basic step, there is much more to be gained in "the way of life" which is recovery. You begin to function as a human being in active responsible ways again.

5.

Recovery

It is obviously impossible to know what resources for help with drinking problems are available in your locality. You will do well to check with the local council on alcoholism if there is one in or near your community—or to consult your doctor or pastor. You need to determine what kind of initial treatment you may need—inpatient, outpatient and/or a direct referral to a group such as Alcoholics Anonymous. We will not discuss the best first step to take, but rather focus on the continuum of recovery. And here we must rely on the group that has taught us more than any other—Alcoholics Anonymous (AA).

Now as soon as we mention AA, we wonder what kind of image forms in your brain, what kind of feelings you start having, and what kind of overall reaction triggers inside of you. Is it something you don't know anything about at all and so you have little or no reaction? Or does it form the image of a bunch of skid row drunks who lost everything through their drinking; a group of religious fanatics; a crowd of misfits who get together once a week to listen to various drinking stories? Does it cause a reaction of "I may have a problem with my drinking but I'm not that bad off" or, "That may be okay for some but it's not for me"?

Perhaps you have been to a good AA meeting or know somebody who is a recovering alcoholic in AA and have primarily good images and feelings about it. Or maybe you have been to a poor meeting— poor because it wasn't a helpful meeting or poor because your mind was closed or your attitude negative and you saw it with distortion. Negative images and responses may be a possibility, but at this point we urge you to consider one suggestion: Keep an open mind. You may end up with the same opinions—but keep an open mind. It is a quite common experience for an alcoholic to go to AA during a time when he is admitting his alcoholism but not fully accepting it. His reaction is very negative. He, and maybe even a professional counselor, may consider that AA is not for him. A permanent judgment made so early is very unwise. In many cases, when such a person is later really accepting his alcoholism, he responds very favorably to AA and actively participates in it as the primary help for continuing sobriety. Whatever your reaction to AA is at this point, remember one thing— alcoholism is a permanent disability that calls for ongoing treatment. As one doctor said "Alcoholism is an illness that needs treatment forever." Recovery involves learning and sustaining a whole new way of life. Because a fellowship like AA also meets this need, good alcoholism treatment programs incorporate AA principles into their philosophy and methods. What we honestly hope is that whatever your knowledge or lack of knowledge about AA, whatever your impressions, feelings and reactions, whether you may need AA now or later, you will give yourself a chance to find out what it really is and make your personal judgment on that basis.

Let's assume that you have taken the "acid test" and made the determination that your drinking has gone into alcoholism. And let's assume that alcoholism is what we have described it to be in Chapter Three. As you give yourself an opportunity to find out what AA suggests as a way of life to sustain recovery from this illness, stack that up honestly against any other possibilities you might have.

Before we get into the way of life that they suggest for recovery we want to say something about the people who are in AA, the nature of their fellowship, and the kind of meetings they hold.

AA is made up of people from all walks of life—educational, economic, vocational, religious, nonreligious. There are people identified with AA who are insincere and people who are very genuine. There are some people who have very serious problems, some with less serious problems, some with many problems, some with few problems. You can find people you will like very much and people you won't like at all—but probably fewer of the latter than in any other group you have ever belonged to. Most are people who know they need you and people who can give much to you. It is one of those groups where alcohol has become the common leveler of all its members. There is no special status. Alcoholics as well as many non-alcoholics who have been exposed to this fellowship feel they have found a reality hard to come by in other groups. It is the kind of fellowship that can meet some basic needs in relationship not only to the drinking problem but to life itself.

If you have the illness of alcoholism, you have experienced a good deal of pain—the pain of estrangement, isolation, guilt, self-hatred, loss of some or all self-respect. That is real pain. In this fellowship you have an opportunity to be a part of a group that has built-in understanding with just the attitudes and relationships that are needed by a person with your kind of pain. One of the more immediate rewards within this fellowship is the beginning of some relief for loneliness and guilt, along with the awareness of hope.

There are basically two kinds of AA meetings—open and closed. Some groups conduct their closed sessions much as they would an open meeting. Usually it is better if the two kinds of meetings are very different.

In meetings open to the public, the customary format is a moment of silence (meditation), a speaker or speakers, the Lord's Prayer, and a social hour. The purpose of this type of meeting is basically three-fold: 1.) To give the beginner a chance to see and hear recovering alcoholics tell their stories in their own way so that he can make identification with both their problem and their recovery and thus begin to feel hopeful; 2.) To give the spouse, friend or community members an opportunity to hear what alcoholism is and does, and what AA is and does; 3.) To inspire and give continuing support for other members of the fellowship. All of this, of course, can also serve to benefit those who speak at the meeting as they are supported by those who listen and respond.

The closed meeting does not usually revolve around a main speaker. It is a real group meeting where in small numbers the members discuss some aspects of the AA way of life as it relates to their own problems and needs. This at its best has the format of silent meditation, a genuine group dynamics session including honest and open exchange, followed by the Lord's Prayer and a social hour. Here a member has the freedom and opportunity to express exactly what he thinks and feels in all candor. Openness, honesty, and frankness are qualities that were strongly present in early AA groups. They are not always present in some groups today. One of the criticisms AA makes of itself is that many closed meetings are primarily "let's be nice to everybody" and not be too candid with each other. Such a meeting is a disservice to those who attend and results in people wearing masks so that the members of the group will not see each other as they really are. If you were to associate with a group lacking these qualities maybe you could help make them a reality. The best kind of meeting allows for education, inspiration, confrontation and support.

Now let us look at the way of life which is recovery. We are not saying that AA is the only place to find this way of life in action, but we are suggesting that generally it is the most available resource in terms of long term help in continuous recovery. It is a way of life, incidentally, that is just as important for the spouse as for the alcoholic. There is a group for spouses called Al-Anon that is usually available in or near most communities.

The reason we included the spouse in the recovery—and have a separate chapter on this subject—is because of the fact that alcoholism is often a family illness. When husband and wife have the problem of alcoholism in their marriage, recovery requires a new and different way of life for both.

When we talk about recovery as a way of life we mean much more than just not drinking. If that were all, and if the alcoholic and his spouse were to go on living together without any change in their attitudes, in their value system, in their behavior, in their relationship with each other, it wouldn't be much of a life—either individually or together.

39

The first requirement that you will be confronted with in this way of life is the need to accept one reality. The immediate focus is upon the dominant reality of your life—loss of control or powerlessness over alcohol, the drinking problem itself. The primary need is to realize and accept the fact that whatever other problems you may think you have, the one you have to concentrate on is the drinking problem because until something is done about that you won't be able to do anything about the others. Alcoholism is an illness that makes a person incapable of being honest with himself until he accepts its presence. His rationalization system prevents facing *any* problems.

Nobody understood the significance of this basic reality until recovering alcoholics in AA stressed it. Telling medicine, psychiatry, psychology, religion and social work this fundamental fact was one of AA's greatest contributions. In a seemingly oversimplified response to an involved problem they broke through all the complexities to provide one vital starting point. If we know ourselves we realize that one of the most natural tendencies is to multiply and magnify our problems to the point where we say, "I have so many problems that even if I wanted to do something about them, I wouldn't know where to begin." That becomes a cagey way to keep ourselves from beginning anyplace. Experience has taught us that if we don't begin someplace we don't begin at all.

In this way of life which is recovery you are asked to break through the multiple-problems picture and see the simple and singular reality of loss of control over alcohol. To accept this reality and to realize that because of this one reality your life is becoming increasingly unmanageable is the beginning of recovery. Someone has said that to ignore this fact and concentrate on resolving other possible underlying causes resembles searching for causes of a fire while the blaze itself goes unchecked.

Once you have seen and accepted this reality, the door can begin to open for you to see and accept other problems about which you will also need to do something. Then and only then, you can begin to see, accept and cope with the other realities of your life.

There is another dimension to this particular focus as a first step towards recovery. As you are confronted with the immediate reality of the drinking problem, you are relieved of the pressure to have answers right now to all the "whys" that may be spinning through your brain. There may be numerous things that you don't yet understand and some that you will never understand, but right now that's not important. Experience has shown that the person who keeps on insisting that he must first find out why he became an alcoholic keeps on drinking. Most of the time the person who is looking for the why is hoping that if he can find that answer, he will somehow be able to regain control and keep on drinking. But he may search forever for the specific answer or answers to the why of "loss of control." Nobody has discovered the cause or causes of the illness.

The second aspect of this way of life is the need for a faith which leads to hope. You will need to *come to believe* (not just think) that there is a power greater than you and your powerlessness who can restore you. It is obvious that if you have come to believe you are actually powerless over alcohol, there is the necessity of coming to believe in a power greater than your powerlessness. Otherwise there can be no hope.

You are asked to begin to say "yes" to the need for help outside yourself. You are not told how to conceive of this greater power or how to believe. The reality of this need is simply presented to you and you are left free to pick it up in whatever way may be possible and meaningful to you. And, incidentally, this spiritual emphasis in the AA way of life meets a basic need in a way that alcoholics ready for recovery tend to respond to quite readily. Alcoholism apparently is an expression, among other things, of some unmet spiritual needs within the person.

To act as if we are the highest and the greatest power is a hard way for any of us to live. For the alcoholic, it is fatal. In that kind of position a person is sitting on the throne of his own life and there is only one way to look and that's down. This posture is a part of the terrible loneliness and hopelessness the alcoholic experiences. Whenever we are on the throne of our own lives, we are unable to look up and see God and also unable to look out to our side and see our family, our friends, our fellowman. As one man said, "It's a wonderful thing to be on the road of recovery and realize that all through the years right beside me was a wife who really cared. I couldn't see her then but I know now that she was always there." So this way of life speaks of the need for a faith that moves from the intellectual level deep down inside. Something has to happen that enables a person to give in, to step off the throne, so he can begin to look up and out and realize that in both directions—divine and human—there is help to be found. It is part of the wisdom of God to extend his help to us through other people.

One of the significant aspects of this part of the new way of life is that no one is telling you how to go about it—because nobody knows or can tell you how. You are asked to start at whatever place and in whatever way you are able at this moment in your life. You don't start with the way someone else understands God or with the way somebody else thinks you ought to understand. You start with the way you understand him—whatever that may be. It means being at the point in your life where you are ready and open to let God meet you at the point of your powerlessness. And many have discovered that it is right at that point that God chooses to meet us.

Coming to faith in God as the source of help and hope, there is the need for commitment, but a new kind of commitment. It is a commitment to a new life, not the way "I want it to be" but "the way God wants it to be for me." This involves the desire and decision to let go the reins and turn your life over to the care of God as you understand him. Aware of the fact that with your own hands on the reins—with yourself in the driver's seat—it hasn't been working out, you are willing to "let go and let God." You may ask "But how do you go about commiting your life to God no matter how you understand him?" Don't wonder about that too much and don't worry about it. If you want this to happen it will happen and you will know what you need to do for now anyway. It may be very limited to begin with but it will be enough. One other aspect of commitment: it is a decision not only to believe but to act, to "bet your life" on your belief. It is in the doing that you experience and learn the validity of this way of life for recovery. A third basic feature of this way of life is the need for honesty about yourself—with yourself, with God and with another human being. It has been demonstrated that there can be no sustained recovery without a significant degree of self-honesty.

The need for self-honesty of course goes unmet unless there is the desire to become honest. Contrary to what many think, self-honesty is not something people generally practice but something they try to avoid. Self-honesty, if it comes at all, usually grows out of pain and crisis. But it is also clear that honesty with ourselves, a basic essential for meaningful existence, is impossible unless we are able to be honest with others and with God. The natural thing for all of us is to point to the defects of other people, to see what is perceived as their failings. It is easy to be critical of others. Indeed, the more guilty and dissatisfied we feel about our own behavior, the more critical we are apt to be of others. In this way of life the focus is upon one's own character defects. The first step is to take a searching, fearless moral inventory. Do you know of someone else who has done this? Chances are you don't. Do you think you have ever really done that? Chances are you haven't. This may be your first real opportunity.

Taking such an inventory involves looking at such realities as: selfishness, alibis, dishonest thinking, pride, lust, resentment, intolerance, impatience, envy, phoniness, procrastination, self-pity, easily hurt feelings, fear. It also involves any particular actions that have been irresponsible, that have caused guilt, that have never been talked out with another person. For the inventory to be of value, it needs to be written out in such a way that it includes some specific examples of each particular defect. Usually this is a painful—not a morbid but a painful—process. We all like to think we don't have these defects but they are common among men. Once we take a good look at them, it isn't so bad. In fact, some of the defects that were once deadly serious business can begin to be looked at with some degree of humor.

In the process of taking the inventory, you are also encouraged to look at some of the good things about yourself—some of the plusses you have going for you. Sometimes the positive aspects of one's person are difficult to perceive and accept at first and are more readily discernible as behavior changes enhance one's own self-esteem.

The self-honesty process involves more than the inventory. It involves admitting to self, God and another human being the exact nature of what has been found. It means sitting with someone else in confidence and saying: this is me, this is the kind of person that I have been. We emphasize another human being because until we are able to admit the truth about ourselves to another person, we have not really admitted it to ourselves or to God. A famous psychiatrist has said that we can only become fully aware of that about ourselves which we are able to admit to another human being. The truth of this statement is learned and understood only through the experience of such self-disclosure. Choosing the person with whom you do this is very important. Some suggest that the best person for this particular kind of self-disclosure is a pastor who understands the process and is the kind of accepting person in whom you can have confidence.

This is the triad of our existence and of our healing—self, God, other people. This is just one type of self-disclosure. It may well be just a part of other self-disclosure going on at the same time or yet to come in the future. For instance, group therapy or an AA meeting is another arena of self-disclosure that has proved to be very valuable for people who have alcoholism.

The person with whom you disclose your inventory needs to be a good listener. When you have finished you should counsel together for clarification, greater understanding, and action that needs to be taken in regard to some of the specific defects that you know are still giving you some trouble.

The experience of inventory and confession should enable you to get to know yourself better, become more keenly aware of how you need to change, recognize the danger signals that could lead to the drinking illness becoming active again, live more comfortably with yourself and others, and have the door opened for a more meaningful relationship with God.

This is an experience that is not only basic in recovery for alcoholism but one that has a positive and meaningful thrust for life itself. It is an experience that is now your opportunity as the direct result of the illness of alcoholism.

The next step along the way of recovery is the desire to change. Without this, of course, the process of seeking self-honesty is of no value. Alcoholism is an illness in which the person not only "does others in," he "does himself in." What is needed is the desire to cease living that kind of self-defeating life.

The only way change will come about in our attitudes and behavior is if deep in our insides we really want to change. There is a great difference between saying "I should change" and really wanting to change. Many people have the idea, or act as though, "should" and "want" are synonymous. Life teaches us that one sure way to avoid change is to continue to think, talk and feel that one *should* change. So it is vital that you become *willing* to change. And you can be sure that if you want to change the attitudes, feelings and behavior that you found as character defects in your inventory, change will take place. When you humbly ask God to help you in overcoming your defects, and act to conquer them, you will begin to experience change not as a negative but a positive experience. It is strange but true that often, without letting ourselves know it, we tend to think that in changing we will lose instead of gain, that doing something about our defects has a negative instead of a positive effect on life. Nothing feels so good and enhances our own self-esteem as much as basic positive change in our attitudes and behavior.

Few human problems hurt other people to the extent that alcoholism does. It insidiously and progressively destroys human relationships. Many alcoholics, while their illness is progressing, are unable to let themselves really see and feel how they are harming themselves and others. When they do realize it, the pain is usually so severe that it immediately gets handled with elaborate rationalization, projection, or denial—and by the anesthesia of alcohol.

So it is that on the road to recovery the alcoholic needs to let himself see the damage that has been done to others. Making a list of people who have been hurt and in what ways is necessary. And then there is the need to make amendment, directly wherever possible. Of course sobriety is the first and primary way of amendment. But to talk with those who have been hurt, to express genuine sorrow, to seek forgiveness, and to express the desire to change, is also important, not only for others but for the alcoholic himself. There really is no other way to heal the pain and brokenness in our relationships. And from the spiritual standpoint there can be no reconciliation with God unless we are reconciled with our fellowman.

One thing you need to be aware of, however: No matter whom you have hurt, there is no one you have hurt more than yourself. To make amendment with yourself is an essential and very difficult step. Here the Serenity Prayer can be helpful. "God grant me the serenity to accept things I cannot change, courage to change things I can, and wisdom to know the difference." One of the graces that comes to many recovering alcoholics is an unrealized capacity to forgive themselves and not to spend their time beating themselves over the head for things they can't change. Part of the process of beginning to be good to yourself is the willingness to forgive yourself.

If you find that little or no progress is being made in this area of recovery then you may have turned to self-pity. By wallowing in self-pity you will be continuing to hold open a door to another drinking episode. One of the most significant results of this part of recovery will be the ability not to take yourself too seriously, the capacity to laugh at yourself—which is one of the freedoms that every human being needs and many never experience.

One aspect of the new way of life is the need for *continued honesty.* Self-honesty is not something we achieve once and then have forever. Self-deception is something that the alcoholic practices so well in the progression of the alcoholism that he can easily revert to it. So there is a need for a daily inventory and when you find yourself wrong to admit it promptly. This is something the alcoholic must pursue "selfishly" because self-deception puts him on the road to drinking, which is for him a life-and-death matter.

So far the way of recovery has involved acceptance of the alcoholism and help for recovery plus basic attitude and behavior change. Now comes the need for continuing spiritual and emotional growth. For the alcoholic growth is essential for continuing sobriety. The suggestion is that you *seek through prayer and meditation to increase your knowledge of God's will for you and to strengthen your power to do it.*

One thing you may or may not be aware of is that when alcoholism came into your life, the possibility of any kind of spiritual or emotional growth was eliminated. The progressive process of alcoholism is inevitably in the opposite direction of growth. With the arresting of the alcoholism, growth once again is a possibility.

Many times when we think of growing (and certainly this is generally true of alcoholics) we have the impatient desire to make giant strides. Actually most growth comes in small and gradual ways. If, for instance, after a period of sobriety you can say honestly that you are a little more patient, that's growth and that's good. If you can begin to say it is getting a little easier for you to put yourself in somebody else's shoes and really know and care how they feel, that's growth. Or if you can more readily "let go and let God," not take yourself so seriously, adopt a more "easy does it" approach, and find yourself with an increasing sense of gratitude, that means you're growing. To be able to be genuinely grateful for little steps is vitally important for continuing growth.

Growth involves the capacity to be reflective about one's own behavior and one's relationship with other people and with God. It calls for a desire to learn to know oneself better and to be less defensive in relationship with others. And there can be no growth without the willingness to take responsible action for changing attitudes and behavior. (There is a little book that many recovering alcoholics find very helpful for their sobriety and their growth. The title is *Twenty-Four Hours a Day* and it can be purchased from Hazelden, Center City, Minnesota, 55012.)

One more thing: It isn't important where you are on the road of growth. What is important is that you are on that road. For instance, here is a man fifty-five years of age just beginning to recover from alcoholism and setting foot on the road to growth. That he is not farther along on the road to growth at his age is no major frustration. That he is on the road of growth, wherever he is, will be a very satisfying experience. It will feel good and be good.

The last step in this way of life for recovery involves the necessity, capacity and willingness to share. Here the exact words used in AA read, "Having had a spiritual awakening as a result of these steps, we tried to carry this message to alcoholics and practice these principles in all our affairs." The only way we can be free to share is first to receive. We cannot give what we do not have. And whatever we receive that is good we will lose if we don't share it.

One of the serious results of alcoholism is the increasing inability to be aware of and responsive to the needs of others as the disease progresses. More and more, alcoholism turns a person in on himself, and increasingly isolates him from himself, others and God. This produces some of the sharpest pain the alcoholic experiences. His estrangement is deepened and his capacity to be a loving person is diminished. The end result, if the alcoholism goes unchecked, is drinking to live and living to drink. To be freed from this kind of bondage is one of the greatest satisfactions in recovery.

On one occasion Paul quotes Jesus as saying, "It is more blessed to give than to receive" (Acts 20:35). But in order to be a truly giving person, we first have to be a receiving person. Many people have never learned to receive comfortably—to let people give to them or to let people help them. It makes them so uncomfortable that they seek to avoid it. Or if they let someone give to them or do something for them, they always feel beholden to that person. They feel the need always to return the favor in some way, and feel discomfort until that can be done.

The initial stance of the recovering alcoholic must of necessity be a receiving one—a willingness to learn from others and receive help from them. As he, through receiving, learns the way of recovery and translates it into action in his own life then he will in turn be able to share with others—not just alcoholics, but also with family and friends.

The carrying of this message and way of life specifically to other alcoholics who have not yet set foot on the road to sobriety is of special importance. By helping those who are suffering from the same illness, the recovering alcoholic finds his own sobriety strengthened.

In living this way of life, the importance of being unable to drink diminishes as the satisfactions of sobriety fill up the vacuum that was left by the removal of drinking. The alcoholic finds himself wanting this new way of life over against the way of life which is alcoholism. Many an alcoholic even finds himself feeling gratitude for the alcoholism because in recovery he has found a way of life he might never have discovered if it weren't for the illness.

Spouse

If you have a drinking problem, you may be surprised that we include in what you are reading a chapter for your spouse. But when you realize that alcoholism is nearly always a family illness, then it makes sense that we ought to talk about this very openly and above board. If your wife is reading this book, we want her to know the facts about alcoholism and recovery and we also want you to know exactly what we have to say to her. Some of what you read in this chapter you may not particularly approve or agree with right now, but nevertheless we want you to have the opportunity to read it too.

If you are the husband or wife of an alcoholic, you may well be the key person in the eventual recovery of the alcoholic. It is important, therefore, that you learn the facts about alcoholism and learn how best to live with and respond to an alcoholic spouse and his illness.

Before proceeding any further it is important for your sake, as well as for the alcoholic's sake, that you learn to accept one truth. You may have had some strong guilt feelings in relation to your spouse's drinking problem. These may have already been intensified by his blaming you for it. It could be that knowingly or unknowingly, by your words, feelings, or behavior, you have been contributing to his drinking problem. But—and this is the important thing for you to realize—you cannot be responsible for his drinking problem and you cannot be responsible for his recovery. Alcoholism is an illness.

You can't produce it in your spouse and you can't arrest it. We do not know why some people lose control over alcohol. We know what needs to be done about it—how to arrest it—and that is and can only be the responsibility of the alcoholic himself.

Your responsibility is to learn about alcoholism, to get help for yourself, and to begin to relate and respond to your alcoholic spouse in ways that hopefully will enhance the possibility of his responsibly seeking help. You also need to know that there is more help and hope for recovery from alcoholism than most people realize.

If you have reacted to the drinking problem by "doing what comes naturally," which you very likely have, then you have reacted in ways that don't help you and can't help the alcoholic. Usually husbands or wives of alcoholics initially respond to the alcoholism in many of the same ways the alcoholic does. The spouse wants to pretend it isn't there, deny it, cover it up, unrealistically hope it will just go away or get better, and then feels more and more angry and guilty about it.

When it becomes obvious that the problem isn't going to go away and can no longer be covered up and is progressively getting worse, then there come attempts to remove it personally. Most spouses begin to respond in ways that have become known as the "home treatment." We include here some examples—and some reasons why they don't work.

1. "Don't you love me? If you really loved me and the children you would do something about your drinking. Don't you realize what you are doing to us and to yourself?" To him, this only communicates lack of understanding of how he feels. He is usually painfully aware of what he is doing. His guilt and self-hatred, his sense of loneliness and rejection, are intensified.

2. "Why don't you be a man? Use your willpower." Imagine what that does to someone who is already overwhelmed with feelings of inadequacy and who has tried, perhaps unbeknown to others, to do just that and failed. This demand only perpetuates an illusion that must be destroyed—the feeling that if he is really a man, he should be able to use his willpower and quit. He needs instead to come to understand that he has a sickness, that

51

this is not a matter of willpower but powerlessness, and that there is nothing shameful or unmanly about accepting this reality and seeking the help he needs for sobriety.

3. Coax him not to drink and try to exact promises. He may make, but cannot keep, promises. His failure then aggravates his guilt, anxiety, and self-hatred. He is supported in his delusion that he can do it on his own if he really tries.

4. Hide or destroy his supply of alcohol. This is a waste of time and money, as the spouse soon learns. The same applies to withholding money and telling friends not to serve him liquor. It is impossible to prevent an alcoholic from getting and drinking alcohol.

5. Threaten him. In most cases the spouse will threaten the alcoholic many times, but never be ready to follow through. He begins to sense that she doesn't really mean it. There is a time when threats can be both necessary and useful. But they should not be used until every other resource has been exhausted.

Frequently spouses react to the alcoholic with a "holier than thou" or martyred attitude. This is not a healthy response for the spouse and cannot help the alcoholic.

As a spouse you need to begin with yourself. Talk with someone who understands alcoholism; a local alcoholism information and referral center, your pastor, maybe your doctor, or someone in Al-Anon. Start attending Al-Anon meetings and read more about alcoholism. Remember alcoholism is an illness and it is important to respond to it as an illness. The appropriate response to illness is to talk with a person who knows about it and can be helpful and in the process to learn about it and what can be done about it.

As you talk with other people who can be helpful you will also have an opportunity to release some of your negative feelings—your anger, frustration, failure, helplessness, hopelessness, self-pity, guilt and fear. Chances are these feelings have been expressed in unhealthy ways for you, your alcoholic spouse and the children. The more you learn about alcoholism and what you can and need to do, the better you will cope with these kinds of feelings.

To let yourself learn that alcoholism is an illness means to see the signs of alcoholism as symptoms of an illness. These you know from your experience in living with an alcoholic (see Chapter 3). These symptoms go with alcoholism as a fever goes with an infection. Because they are behavioral symptoms like denial, alibi, rationalization, minimization, projection of the reason for drinking on you or someone else, refusal to talk about it, lying, etc., they are more difficult to accept as symptoms than accepting a high temperature. But once you can accept them as such, they cease to be the threat and source of anger and frustration that they have been. You will realize that he can't respond any differently until he understands and accepts his alcoholism. You will realize that if alcoholism ever came into your life you would respond and behave just the way he does.

As the alcoholism progresses the alcoholic develops unreasonable resentments and quite often lashes out at the people to whom he is closest. If you have already experienced this you no doubt have found yourself feeling guilty and responding defensively—as if it were really true that you are to blame for his drinking problem. When you can accept this as a symptom of the illness, however, you can let it be. You won't feel guilty. You won't be defensive. You won't need to try to prove him wrong. You can just let him live with what he says and does. And in case he forgets, then, in a quiet moment when he is sober you may want to ask him, without accusation or anger, "Do you remember what you said to me and did last night?" If he says no, you will want to recall it for him so he will not be able to avoid one of the results of his drinking problem.

This leads into a very important area. The alcoholic needs to be treated in a way that allows him to experience as fully as possible all the natural results of his drinking. We call this "surrounding the alcoholic with the reality of his alcoholism." There are enough problems connected with alcoholism without imposing any more so that if he is allowed to experience all of them, the day when he is ready to seek help can in most cases be significantly hastened.

To pamper your spouse or cover up for him can only do harm and delay recovery. Because of the nature of alcoholism, he will only use such responses to manipulate you, further avoid his alcoholism, and continue his drinking. If he can't make it to work on Monday morning, don't call the boss for him. If there is going to be any lying, don't lie for him. He has the Monday morning problem because of his drinking. Let it be his problem. If creditors start calling, no matter what reason he gives you for the bills not being paid, you ask them to get in touch with your husband. You know that the reason for unpaid bills is his drinking. If he gets picked up for drunken driving, let that be his problem entirely. And in these and other situations resulting from his drinking, tell him calmly, without hostility, that the problems exist because of his drinking and therefore *he* is going to have to deal with them. Don't argue about it. Just tell him honestly what you think and how you feel.

You will also do well not to tolerate any physical abusiveness (if it gets to that) or any drunken sexual relations. Although it may become increasingly difficult, sexual relations can still be a part of the marriage when he is sober.

It is also important that you not allow your alcoholic spouse to lie to you and have you accept it as truth. Remember, he can't help lying. It is one of the symptoms that inevitably goes with alcoholism. The truth is always painful, but try as best you can to have him face the truth. Remember too that if he can outsmart you, manipulate you, deceive you, take advantage of you, he will naturally do so, and that will only result in further evasion for him and less respect for you.

By helping him to face the facts, you move him closer to accepting his problem and seeking help. Sometimes, however, it reaches the point where firmer action becomes necessary—a serious either-or situtaion: Either he goes for help or he will no longer be able to live with you and the children. Before you take this step you must make sure that it is your carefully considered decision to set such a limit, that you are not doing it out of resentment but rather to further surround your spouse with the realities of his alcoholism, and that you are ready to follow through firmly.

How is the alcoholic apt to respond to your getting help for yourself, learning about alcoholism, changing your attitudes and responses? At first this will probably make him quite angry. Initially it may baffle him and he may make various efforts to try to get you to revert to your old patterns. For as long as the alcoholic has his spouse on the defensive, he has it going his way. But as you persevere in your determination to let go and let the alcoholism really be his problem, he will on some level pick this up as your real care and concern for him. To put it another way, you are helping to provide the kind of emotional climate in which the possibility of his seeking help is enhanced.

In this whole process of learning and getting help for yourself, you will have to decide when is the best time for you actually to say to your husband that you think his drinking has gone into alcoholism. There is no reason to avoid saying this once you are quite convinced it is time. You will, however, want to share this with him when he isn't drinking and in a way that may cause him to hear clearly and reflect seriously on what you say.

Your understanding, attitudes and responses to the alcoholism will need to be learned also by your children. It is very important that they see and accept this as an illness. That will make it easier for them to live with the behavior of the alcoholic parent, which otherwise severely confuses and hurts them. Usually the better you learn to live with it, the better they will. And sometimes a child can get through to an alcoholic parent when a spouse can't.

There is help for you and your family. Perhaps a local clinic or counseling service. One of the best resources for help is Al-Anon. Very likely there is a group in your area. Al-Anon is a fellowship for spouses and adult family members or relatives of the alcoholic. In this fellowship you meet others who are living with alcoholics, some of them still drinking and some on the road to recovery. They can readily identify with and understand what you are experiencing. You will no longer feel all alone. Al-Anon exists not to help the alcoholic but to help you with your problems. The members can help you toward acceptance of your powerlessness over the drinking problem and toward changing your attitudes and behavior. As you continue in Al-Anon, you in turn will be able to help others. Besides attending

Al-Anon meetings, it would be a good idea also to attend some open AA meetings. If you feel that you need further help, seek out a competent counselor if you can. There is Alateen for the teen-agers. If there is an Alateen in or near your community, encourage any teen-agers you have to attend. If there isn't an Alateen maybe you can be helpful in getting a group started.

Once the alcoholic is moving towards recovery, it is important that you support him in his efforts, but not do for him what he needs to do for himself. In the initial phase of recovery if he accepts AA, he may live and sleep AA. Give this time. If you are active in Al-Anon, that will help during this period. In time life should settle down to more normality as his need to live and sleep AA diminishes.

The importance of both alcoholic and spouse being involved in recovery is underscored by the fact that once there is sobriety, there may well be problems, marital and otherwise, that have been ignored or avoided because of the alcoholism. It just isn't realistic to expect that once the drinking ceases, everything will be fine. You may discover that marital counseling is needed.

Everything we have been saying here is with the assumption that you will be open to learn and benefit from the help that is available. There are some spouses who have a hidden need to be married to a drinking alcoholic. No doubt you have heard stories of the woman who divorces an alcoholic husband saying "Never again" and in a short time is married to another one. This kind of person may have excessive needs to dominate, control, punish, suffer, or feel needed. If you find that you are not benefiting from the kind of help we have been talking about, then you would do well to seek more professional help.

If your spouse recovers and begins to grow and you do not, very serious problems can develop. But if both of you, individually and together, are working on the problems, then out of the estrangement and pain of alcoholism there can come, by the grace of God, a new kind of life for which you will both feel forever grateful.